Original Designs
for Smocking

MILNER CRAFT SERIES

Original Designs for Smocking

JENNY BRADFORD

SALLY MILNER PUBLISHING

First published in 1992 by
Sally Milner Publishing Pty Ltd
558 Darling Street
Rozelle NSW 2039 Australia

Reprinted 1994

© Jenny & Don Bradford, 1992

Design concept by David Constable
Design layout by Gatya Kelly, Doric Order
Illustrations by Don Bradford
Photography by Andre Martin
Typeset in Australia by Asset Typesetting Pty Ltd
Printed in Australia by Impact Printing, Melbourne

National Library of Australia Cataloguing-in-Publication data:

Bradford, Jenny, 1936-
   Original designs for smocking.

   ISBN 1 86351 087 7.

   1 .Smocking. I. Title. (Series : Milner craft series).

746.44

Other MILNER CRAFT SERIES books
by Jenny Bradford

Silk Ribbon Embroidery for Gifts and Garments
Bullion Stitch Embroidery
Original Designs for Silk Ribbon Embroidery
Textured Embroidery

ACKNOWLEDGEMENTS

Iam indebted to Sue Batterham and Jan Kerton for their continual advice and support during the preparation of this book, for their designs that are published in the book and the beautiful garments that they have sewn for me.

Sue, a former student of mine, and a gifted designer, has a wonderful ability to produce lovely design plates that are refreshingly different and include some clever combinations of stitches.

Jan, owner of Windflower Smocking in Melbourne, is an expert teacher and gifted sewer. I know her charming designs will appeal to both beginners and advanced students alike.

A special thank you to Judi Anders, owner of Tiffany's Porcelain Art Studio, Melbourne, Victoria, for making the beautiful Hilda reproduction doll for Jan to dress. Also to Elena Dickson for the lovely lace edging she worked on the blouse collar, a design from her beautiful book, *Knotted Lace*, published by Sally Milner Publishing.

My thanks as always to my husband, Don, who has in the process of preparing this book spent endless hours graphing the design plates by computer with, I hope you will agree, great success. Without Don's support in the time consuming tasks of drawing diagrams, word processing and proof reading I would almost certainly never attempt to produce a book at all.

I also thank the following businesses for their support and donation of supplies:

Bernina Australia Pty Ltd,
Castle Hill, NSW
    — for the Amanda Jane pleater

Cotton On Creations,
Bowral, NSW
    — for fabrics and lace

Minnamurra Threads,
Glebe, NSW
    — for hand dyed variegated thread

Stadia Handicrafts,
Paddington, NSW
    — for Au Ver A Soie threads

Windflower Smocking,
Moonee Ponds, Victoria
    — for fabric

CONTENTS

Acknowledgements   vii
Introduction   1
1 Tools and Techniques   2
2 Sophisticated Smocking   9
3 Design Plates   22
   — Alice   15
   — Alice Minor   16
   — Alice Minimus   17
   — Amanda's Christening   18
   — Antique Lace   19
   — Baby Fiona   21
   — Britanny's Bishop   22
   — Bunnies, Beads and Bows   24
   — Carnival   25
   — Hearts and Flowers   27
   — Kaleidoscope   29
   — Karen   31
   — Laura   32
   — Lisa   34
   — Margaret   35
   — Pattie   37
   — Baby Pattie   38
   — Pauline   38
   — Tudor Rose   40
Smocking Plaids
   Practical plaids   44
Stacking Designs for Picture Smocking
   — Alphabet   47
   — Butterfly — large   49
   — Butterfly — small   50
   — Dolphin   50
   — Hearts 'My Love'   51
   — Sea Plane—   53
4 Stitch Glossary   54

INTRODUCTION

Smocking design plates are extremely important to all smocking enthusiasts. They are the key to making every item that you make look different, even though the same basic construction pattern is used time and time again.

Choosing a design to enhance the fabric selected is part of the art of creating a masterpiece for everyone to admire. This book contains twenty-eight graphed designs for every level of ability. Add to this the possibilities of working some of those designs with or without beads and ribbon threading, substituting bullions for flowerettes and vice-versa and the variations possible from the basic designs given are greatly extended.

A section on counterchange smocking using plain fabrics is included, along with ideas for using Van Dyke stitch and backsmocking to create fancy yokes and feature panels for sophisticated adult garments.

Helpful hints on smocking, pleating machines and a stitch glossary complete what will, I trust, be a useful and well used smocking book for your library.

Jenny Bradford 1992

CHAPTER ONE

TOOLS AND TECHNIQUES

PLEATING

Currently there are several pleaters available on the market. They are small hand-operated machines designed to put the pleating threads into the fabric in the shortest time. It is not possible to do this process on an ordinary sewing machine.

If you do not do sufficient smocking to warrant the purchase of a machine, your local needlecraft shop, embroiderers' guild or a private teacher may operate a pleating service.

The following list details the main brands of pleating machines available here in Australia. As with choosing any mechanical device it is best to look around at the various options and make a choice according to your own personal needs.

AMANDA JANE

Made in Australia and distributed by Bernina Australia Pty Ltd, Castle Hill, NSW.

A 24 row pleater with ½ space needles between 12 rows.

Easy and comfortable to use, the master roller is held in place with a pin device and does not require the use of a screwdriver to remove the needles.

The pleating threads pass through close to the centre of the pleat and there is little or no difference in the depth of the pleating threads on the right and wrong sides.

SALLY STANLEY

Made in South Africa and distributed in Australia by Country Bumpkin, Norword, South Australia.

A 24 row pleater with ½ space needles between the first 8 rows.

This pleater is easy and comfortable to use. A screwdriver is necessary to remove and replace the main roller. The needles are interchangeable with the Amanda Jane.

The pleating threads will be positioned so that when looking at the right side of the fabric, they are lower down and closer to the base of the pleat than those on the Amanda Jane, provided the fabric is passed through the machine in the correct way.

READ PLEATERS

Made in South Africa and distributed in Australia by MSC Distributors Pty Ltd, Melbourne, Victoria.

This is the only pleater available in three different sizes:

- a small 16 row model with ½ space needles between 6 rows;
- a 24 row model with ½ space needles between 12 rows;
- a 32 row model with ½ space needles between 17 rows.

No screwdriver is required for the larger models. Needles vary according to the machine, and the needles used in the larger machines are a little more fragile than those used in other pleaters.

Whichever pleater you choose, make sure you know how to dismantle it completely so that you can clean the ends of the rollers regularly.

The rollers should turn smoothly and easily when tested without fabric. Always remove needles not required for the project in hand and never use a distorted needle in the machine; it is the quickest way to break needles.

Prepare the fabric for pleating carefully. Pre-wash, remove selvedges and ensure the panels are on the straight grain of the fabric. Never cut armhole or other shaping prior to pleating. Mark cutting lines with a fabric pen, leaving a straight edge to be fed into the rollers.

A bishop style garment must be constructed from a pattern designed for a pleating machine. The armhole shaping on the front, sleeves and back are cut so that when they are sewn together prior to pleating they form a straight yoke section that is easily passed through the pleating machine.

Very fine fabrics may pleat more successfully if a spray starch is used prior to pleating. Synthetic fabrics and fine wool may resist pleating and bubble. Try using half space pleating, if possible. Remove the pleats from the needles carefully, keeping them in a solid block as you slide them on to the threads. After pleating, draw up the threads tightly and pin the panel, stretching it vertically to hold the pleats in place, steam well and allow to dry before preparing for smocking.

Always pleat an extra row above and below the design to facilitate easy working of the first and last rows of the design.

Backsmocking with cable along one or both of these rows will assist in the process of mounting the panel or applying a neck binding.

Always leave the pleating threads in the row to be used for mounting neck bindings or yokes until the garment is assembled.

PLEATING BY DOTS

It is still possible to purchase transfer dots for pleating fabric by hand. These dots can be used on any pattern, including a bishop style garment designed for a pleating machine.

When pleating fabric with these dots, iron them on to the wrong side of the material and pleat the fabric by picking up each dot in turn, resulting in a small stitch on the front of the work and a longer stitch on the back of the work.

FABRIC ALLOWANCE

The accepted basic rule is three times the finished width of the required panel. This does, however, vary according to the weight of the fabric, the density of the pattern and the type of stitches to be used.

Three times the finished width applies to an average weight cotton fabric of the type used for everyday summer weight garments. A very fine voile or batiste will require 3½ to 4 times the finished width, whereas a winter weight cotton or very fine corduroy will require 2¼ to 3 times the finished width.

Stitches such as honeycomb, Van Dyke and counterchange require less fabric allowance, provided they are used on their own and not mixed with bands of cables, waves, etc. Stacking designs do not have the elasticity of regular smocking designs and therefore take up more fabric if distortion of the finished result is to be avoided.

Note that there are some commercial patterns produced that are smocked without pre-pleating. The design is produced by ironing dots onto the right side of the fabric and working the pattern by picking up the dots in a set sequence. These patterns do not allow sufficient fabric to pre-pleat the panel prior to smocking.

THREADS

The choice of threads is many and varied. My advice to students is always to use a thread that you enjoy handling and one that gives you a pleasing result.

The designs photographed for this book have been worked in a variety of threads in order to show a range of possibilities. Note that the thickness of the thread used varies according to the weight of the fabric being worked.

STRANDED COTTON THREAD

The most versatile and commonly used, being readily available in a wide range of colours. The number of strands used may vary according to the fabric; 2 or 3 strands are generally used but 4 may be used for stacking designs.

VARIEGATED STRANDED COTTON THREAD

There is an increasing range of these threads available and I find them exciting to use. These threads may well be the perfect answer for those who find colour mixing a difficult task, as one skein of a pleasing colour blend will give sufficient colour variation for a complete design (see 'Alice' on colour plate 3). They work up best on plain colour backgrounds and can be used to advantage in some stacking designs (see the hearts design and the initials on colour plate 5). Most of the variegated threads used in the designs illustrated are from a small but lovely selection of hand-dyed stranded cotton from Minnamurra Threads of Sydney, NSW.

MARLITT

(Also available as Decora)
A very shiny viscose stranded thread which you will either love or hate! Static can be removed to a degree by pulling the threaded needle through an anti-static pad designed for use in a clothes drier or by ironing with a steam iron. I do not recommend using the thread damp or waxing with beeswax. Two strands are usually sufficient and easier to handle than three and a single strand makes lovely delicate bullion rose buds.

AU VER A SOIE

A stranded silk thread beautifully smooth and easy to use; one of my favourites for stacking, as three strands are equivalent to four of stranded cotton and easier to work.

SOIE GOBELIN

A silk buttonhole twist thread which I find works very well for stitches such as Van Dyke on fine voile (see yoke panel in the colour section).

COTON PERLÉ (PEARL COTTON)

No. 8 is usually heavy enough for most smocking. This is a shiny cotton thread with a definite twist and very easy to use, as a single strand is sufficient.

It is necessary to use a knot in the thread to start the work, so try to avoid too many joins across a panel as these may show once the pleating threads are withdrawn.

If the necessary length of thread is too difficult to handle, try starting the work in the centre of the panel, leaving half the length of thread hanging at the back. Complete half the row with the threaded needle, return to the centre, turn the work upside down, re-thread the needle with the other half of the thread and complete the row.

Always remember when using stranded threads to strip the thread before threading the needle. Separate each individual thread by pulling up in the line of the threads as shown in the diagram. Smooth them back together and then thread in the needle.

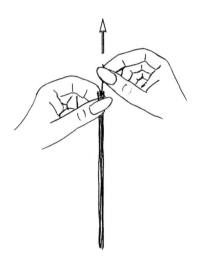

NEEDLES

Crewel needles are generally used for smocking. The size will vary according to the thickness of the thread used and the density of the weave of the fabric.

Any needle used for embroidery should pierce a hole in the fabric large enough for the threaded eye of the needle to pass through easily and smoothly without having to be pulled unnecessarily hard. Resistance such as this can be responsible for aching fingers and even cause RSI or 'tennis elbow'. It is also worth remembering that if the thread is cramped too much the strands will not easily spread out and lay smoothly and evenly across the pleats, which is particularly noticeable when working stacking designs.

ADJUSTING PLEATS FOR SMOCKING

Pleating threads must be tied off before smocking is started. Adjusting the tension of the pleats usually causes beginners some concern. The main thing is to set up your work so that it is comfortable for you. The following points may help you to adjust the pleats to suit you.

Consider the factors that have a bearing on the evenness and tension of your stitching:

- You must be able to *see* the pleating threads as you work in order to maintain accurate spacing.
- The needle must pick up each pleat at the same depth to maintain even tension.
- The needle must pass through each pleat at right angles to that pleat to maintain the correct angle of the stitches.

If the pleating threads are tied off too tightly it will be impossible to separate the pleats sufficiently to work in this way. If the threads are too loose the pleats will be too sloppy to maintain an even tension.

Remember the pleats can be moved along the pleating threads as required and there should be just enough room to do this in order to separate out each pleat as you stitch.

CHOICE OF DESIGN

The size of the design should be in direct proportion to the size of the garment, particularly when smocking bishop style garments.

The depth of the design should form a yoke, i.e. take up the distance between the neckline of the garment and the point of the shoulder and not extend down into the sleeve area.

All bishop style designs finish with a row of waves and *never* with a straight row of cables. The depth of the waves should be in direct proportion to the depth of the smocking, e.g. a six or seven row design will finish with small waves; a deep design, 10 rows or more used on a larger garment, must finish with deeper waves worked over two or even three spaces.

Fabric can play a part in the choice of design; heavily patterned fabrics such as Liberty prints will need a heavily smocked design for it to show up on the background. Stacking designs are more difficult to work on lightweight fabrics, such as voile or batiste, as they do not have enough body to support the density of stitching involved.

BLOCKING

To block or steam the finished smocking, remove all pleating threads except those required as mounting guides (usually the top thread and sometimes the bottom one if the panel is to be mounted at both edges). Pin the work out to size, taking care to pin the design evenly and ensuring the pleats are kept on the correct line. To set the pleats, steam with a hot iron held just above the work. Insufficient blocking can cause a yoke to pucker across the seam line or a bishop garment to 'stand up' like a tube around the neckline.

CHAPTER TWO

SOPHISTICATED SMOCKING

Istill find it hard to persuade students that smocking can be used to embellish garments other than lingerie for the adult wardrobe.

As we get older and maybe our figures are less than perfect, the thought of the extra fullness created by the pleats associated with smocking does not appeal to our sense of fashion. A popular solution is to use the smocking to create texture that can be incorporated into yokes, panels or cuffs, making it a feature of blouses, dresses or jackets.

Colour plates show examples of both finished garments and constructed yokes ready for assembly. This method of smocking is often most effective if worked in the same colour as the base fabric, using texture, e.g. shiny threads on a dull fabric, rather than the contrast of colour for definition.

The most suitable designs for this type of work are those which use stitches requiring a minimum of fullness. Honeycomb, Van Dyke or counterchange smocking are all effective and easy to use.

GENERAL INSTRUCTIONS

Adapting patterns for the insertion of smocked counterchange or Van Dyke panels is very easy, because the smocking, once completed and blocked, is not heavy or bulky. The panels are easy to work with and will not distort the drape of the garment if positioned correctly.

The method of construction used enables a panel to be inserted in many different ways, allowing for easy adaption of a variety of dressmaking patterns.

The principle used will be familiar to heirloom sewing and patchwork enthusiasts; it involves joining strips of fabric together to make a piece large enough from which to cut out the required pattern shape.

Any simple shape such as a yoke, large collar, panels, sleeves, cuffs or jacket pieces can be constructed in this way.

For the most effective results, choose garment patterns with simple, uncluttered lines and position panels carefully so that they do not conflict with shaping darts, pleats or gathers.

The fabric panels used to join the smocked panels can be embellished with tucks, lace or embroidery. Lace beading or entredeux threaded with ribbon can add to the decorative effect and at the same time cover up what can be a rather unsightly seam if lightweight fabric is used for the garment. A lace edging can be used for the same purpose. (See yoke pictured in the colour section).

Embroidered decoration can be added according to taste. Instructions for these and other suitable ribbon embroidery flowers may be found in *Bullion Stitch Embroidery, Silk Ribbon Embroidery for Gifts and Garments* and *Original Designs for Silk Ribbon Embroidery.*

TUCKS

To make straight, even tucks, ensure panels are cut on the straight by drawing a thread to mark the cutting line. Draw a thread along the fold line of each tuck. Fold and press, using spray starch for a firm sewing surface. Sew using the inner edge of the machine foot as a guide, adjusting the needle position to left or right for more or less width.

Mock tucks can be made by working straight lines of sewing using a twin needle in the machine.

PREPARING A PANEL FOR CONSTRUCTING A GARMENT

Once the fabric is pieced together, block and press carefully.

Lay the pattern piece on the fabric, taking care to centre the panels where necessary. Pin in place and mark the outline of the pattern piece on to the panel carefully.

Remove the pattern piece and sew around the marked outline, with the machine set for a long straight stitch.

Sew around a second time just inside the original outline.

Using a wide zigzag stitch, sew around the panel a third time, working over the second stitching line and just inside the first row of straight stitching.

Cut out the panel along the first stitching line.

Continue garment construction as directed in the pattern.

Important points to remember when working smocking for this type of decoration are:

- Lightweight fabrics are the most successful for panels.
- The edges must be kept straight to facilitate even mounting.
- Where panels are turned around (counterchange panels) work an extra row of cable on either side of the panel to be used as a stitching guide when mounting.
- For a smooth fit, this work is usually pinned out and blocked to remove all stretch from the panel prior to mounting. As stretching the work in this way will have an effect on the finished width or length of the panel, be sure to allow for this in your calculations.

COUNTERCHANGE SMOCKING

Many readers may remember smocking on check gingham fabrics to make cushions, sun hats and aprons. Most of these items were made using the counterchange method of smocking. The squares of the fabric were used as a guide for picking up the pleats and the design could be completed without the time consuming process of pre-pleating the fabric. This type of smocking is currently enjoying a great deal of popularity owing to the production of specially designed fabrics with *even* checks or stripes incorporated in their design. Even stripes can be used by drawing lines across the panels to use as a stitching guide.

The finished design worked on this type of fabric depends on the pick up points coming exactly in line with the colour lines on the fabric. The finished work then consists of blocks of colour forming the design. For example, if working on a pink and white striped fabric, it is possible to work in such a way that the stitching will cause the main design, such as hearts, to appear in pink and the background area to show in white. There are design plates available for this type of smocking, together with specially designed imported fabrics. Information on these supplies should be available from shops specialising in smocking supplies.

The counterchange smocking suggestions used in this book do not require special fabrics but are worked on pre-pleated panels. This gives a much wider choice of fabrics, allowing the use of fine cotton and/or polyester for pretty but practical garments such as blouses, brunch coats and lingerie.

Some of the advantages of this type of smocking are:

- Counterchange requires only twice the finished width of the fabric and is therefore much less bulky than regular smocking.
- There is no stretch in counterchange, making it ideal for garment panels.
- It is easy and quick, being based on rows of cable and requiring less fullness. An ideal choice if you wish to cover a few coathangers for presents or fund raising.

- It actually works better on a poly/cotton mixture, making garment laundering easy.
- The flat finish of the pleats is easier to embellish with embroidery than regular smocking.

All the counterchange panels used in the items illustrated are worked with rows of cable spaced at each full space pleating thread as shown in the diagram. It is possible to vary the spacing from ½ up to 1½ space rows as desired. The only essential point to remember is that a bottom level cable on one row *must* always line up with a top level cable on the row below.

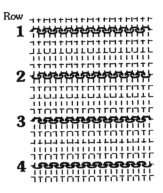

Counterchange Blouse
Designed and made by Jenny

A plain shirt style with a small yoke section over the shoulder line will be the easiest to use. Smock two panels with about seven rows of cable; white Coton Perlé No. 8 is very suitable for this purpose. When stretched and blocked, these panels should fit the length of the front blouse pattern pieces. (Remember the fourth point of 'Preparing a Panel for Constructing a Garment'.) Sew a panel of fabric down each side of the smocked pieces to make panels large enough from which to cut the blouse fronts according to the pattern. Care should be taken to line up and centre the smocked panel accurately when cutting out the blouse fronts.

Trim the joining seams with lace beading threaded with ribbon. A tiny colonial knot worked in 4 mm silk ribbon is worked at regular intervals down the ribbon insertion.

Straight stitch ribbon rose buds are worked over the counterchange down the centre of the panel.

Finish construction of the garment as detailed in the pattern.

The blouse illustrated is made in polyester/cotton voile.

Counterchange Yoke _____
Designed and made by Jenny

This panel is built up from smocked strips and decorated with mock tucks and clusters of bullion stitch daisies. The smocking is worked in white Coton Perlé No. 8 and the seams decorated with a narrow white lace edging. This panel could be used for a nightgown or brunch coat or any garment with a square yoke. The panel illustrated is made in a lightweight polyester/cotton fabric.

Shaped Blouse Yoke _____
Designed and made by Jenny

The yoke is constructed from panels of Van Dyke stitch worked across 18 pleats; these are joined with plain fabric panels cut to match the width of the lace used to overlay each plain panel. The fabric is very fine Swiss batiste. When the piecing is completed, the panel is backed with a second layer of fabric before the lace panels are sewn in place through both layers. The yoke is then prepared according to the instructions below.

Dress Yoke _____
Designed and made by Jenny

If the complete yoke is smocked as shown on the dress (see colour section), a neater finish will be achieved if the lower edge of the yoke is pre-finished prior to pleating, either with a rolled hem edge, lace or by pressing under a hem and securing it in the first row of pleating.

The yoke pieces for this garment are backsmocked using three-pleat Van Dyke stitch (see glossary). After smocking, block carefully before marking, sewing and cutting as described.

When constructing the garment, cut a yoke lining and reverse the usual construction procedure by attaching the yoke lining to the bodice pieces and overlaying the outer yoke, which is then hand sewn over the seam line along the lower edge.

It may be necessary to tack the smocking to the yoke lining at intervals if it does not sit perfectly.

Fresh water pearls have been used for a special touch of decoration on the surface. The fabric is a lightweight cotton/polyester chosen for the interesting effect pleating has on the fabric design.

CHAPTER THREE

DESIGN PLATES

GENERAL INFORMATION

Commence all designs by centring with the stitch and row indicated on the graphs by the arrow.

It is important to centre a design so that it starts and finishes at the same point of the design across the panel. Care should be taken to position the point or valley of the wave row of a bishop design in the centre front of the bishop garment, otherwise the finished garment may have a lop-sided look.

All the graphs have the centring row marked with a $\gg$ and the centre stitch of that row indicated with an arrow.

When starting a design in the middle of the pattern it is easier and safer to continue working row by row away from that point. This greatly reduces the possibility of errors causing mis-matching of the pattern.

- The stitches used for the design are listed with the graphs; details of how to work these stitches will be found in the stitch glossary at the back of the book.

- Read the graphs carefully to ensure that top and bottom stitches line up as indicated, otherwise the pleats will not line up exactly as shown in the colour plates.

- Backsmocking should be worked to prevent puffing of pleats where the gaps in the surface stitching exceed one full pleating space.

- When working on ½ space pleating, it is easier if threads of a different colour are used for ½ and full space rows when threading the pleater.

- Design plates have been graded as far as possible, to indicate the degree of difficulty, as follows:

★ Very Easy   ★★★ Intermediate
★★ Easy   ★★★★ Advanced

References are made to both silk ribbon embroidery and bullion stitch embroidery in some of the instructions. Further instructions on silk ribbon embroidery can be found in my books *Silk Ribbon Embroidery for Gifts and Garments* and *Original Designs for Silk Ribbon Embroidery*. Further information on bullion stitch embroidery and the silk threads 'Kanagawa 1000' and

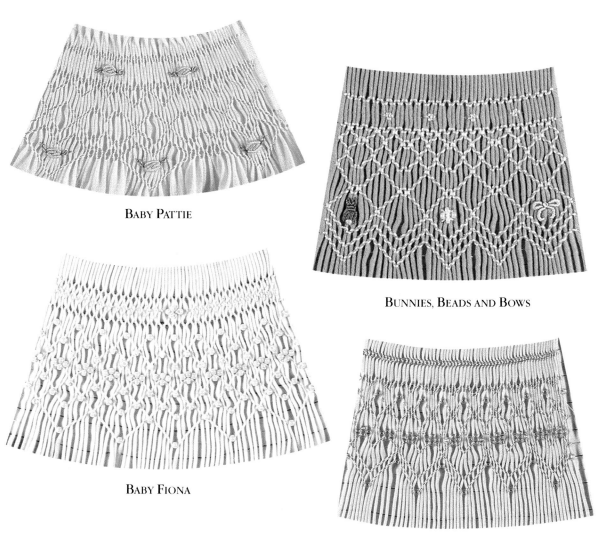

BABY PATTIE

BUNNIES, BEADS AND BOWS

BABY FIONA

AMANDA'S CHRISTENING

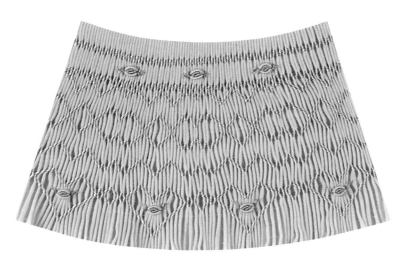

PATTIE

PLATE 1 — BISHOP DESIGNS

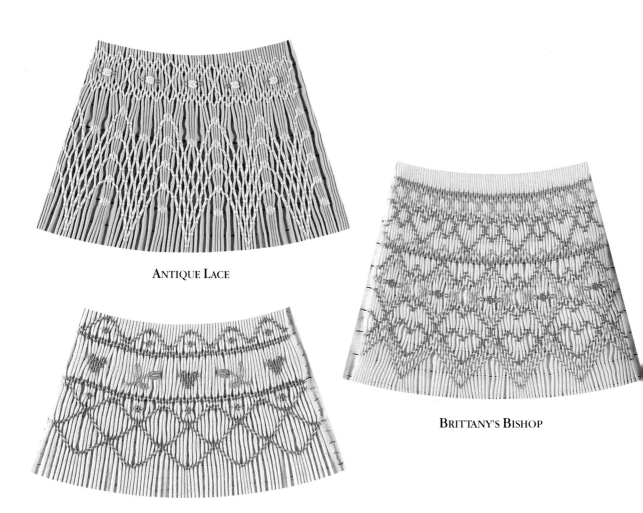

ANTIQUE LACE

BRITTANY'S BISHOP

HEARTS AND FLOWERS

PAULINE

PLATE 2 — BISHOP DESIGNS

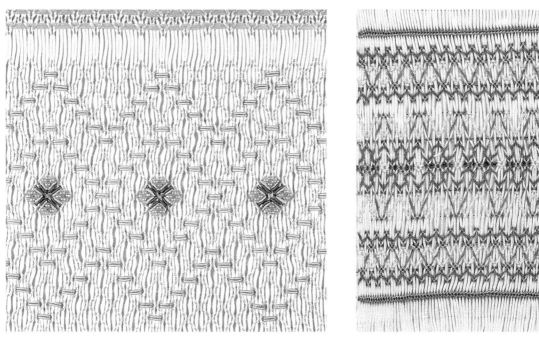

MARGARET

CARNIVAL

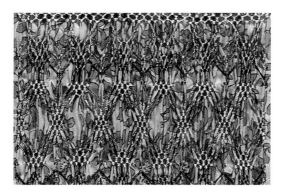

KALEIDOSCOPE

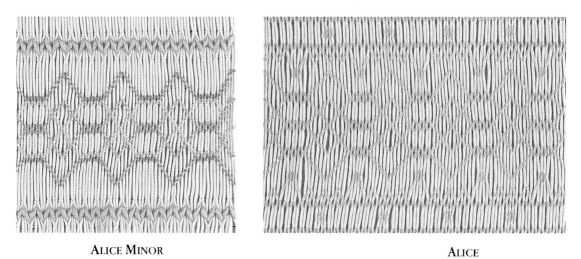

ALICE MINOR

ALICE

PLATE 3 – STRAIGHT DESIGNS

TUDOR ROSE

LAURA

HEARTS AND FLOWERS

LISA

KAREN

PLATE 4 – STRAIGHT DESIGNS

'Silk Stitch' that have also been referenced in this book
can be found in my book *Bullion Stitch Embroidery*.

Alice ★★
Designer — Jenny Bradford

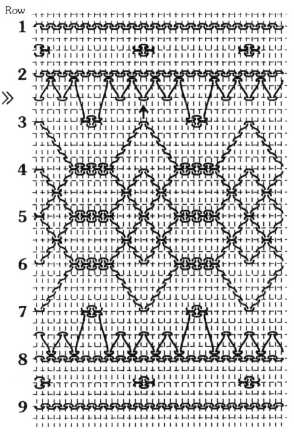

Row 1	cable
Row 2	cable — mirror image of Row 1
≫ Row 2-3	½ and full space chevrons with double flowerettes
Row 3-4	5 step full space wave with 7 cable blocks
Row 4-4½	2 step ½ space wave with 7 cable blocks
Row 4½-5	mirror image of Row 4-4½
Rows 5-6	repeat Rows 4-5
Row 6-7	5 step full space wave with 7 cable blocks
Rows 7-9	mirror image of Rows 1-3
Row 1½ & 8½	double flowerettes

Centre Row 2-3; centre stitch — middle cable on Row 2½ of a block of 3 chevrons.

This design can be enlarged by adding further repeats of Rows 5-6 before continuing with Row 6-7.

The original design was worked with Minnamurra hand-dyed stranded cotton colour number 80/2.

Alice Minor and Alice Minimus ★★★

These are two versions of Alice with a border featuring an attractive form of ribbon threading. Half space pleating will make working easier. There is a subtle difference when the rows are worked in the order shown on the graphs and as listed below.

Alice Minor

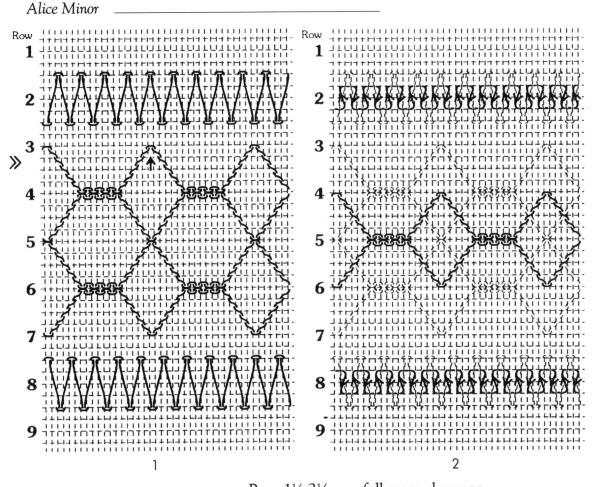

1

2

Row 1½-2½	full space chevrons
≫ Row 3-4	5 step full space wave with 7 cable blocks (graph 1)
Row 4-5	mirror image of Row 3-4 (graph 1)
Rows 5-7	repeat Rows 3-5 (graph 1)
Row 4-6	5 step full space wave with 7 cable blocks (graph 2)
Row 7½-8½	mirror image of Row 1½-2½

Centre Row 3-4; centre stitch — top level cable Row 3

Using 4 mm wide pure silk ribbon, thread the chevron rows with ribbon, carefully following the direction of the arrows shown on graph 2.

Alice Minimus

This is similar to Alice Minor but with Rows 4-6 worked in a different order.

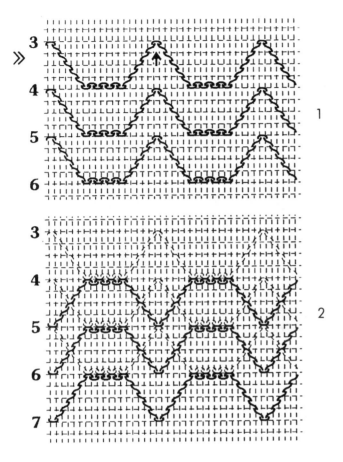

Work Rows 3-6 all in the same direction (graph 1).

Work Rows 4-7 all in the same direction (graph 2).

Interesting colour combinations can be achieved with the overlapping of the rows.

Amanda's Christening ★
Designer — Jan Kerton

A charming bishop design that looks equally good with or without the addition of tiny beads.

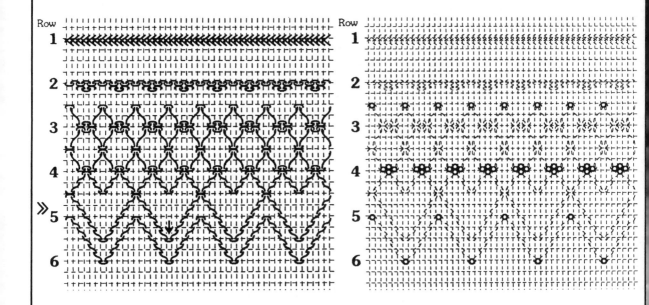

Row 1	stem/outline stitch
Row 2	cable plus second row of cable with skipped pleats (thread carried across back of work)
Row 2½-4	3 rows ½ space baby wave with 3 cables to form double flowerettes on Row 3; single flowerettes on Row 4
Row 4-4½	2 step ½ space wave
≫ Row 4½-5½	5 step full space wave
Row 5-6	5 step full space wave

Centre Row 4½-5½; centre stitch — bottom cable Row 5½ in centre of heart

Beads are added on the top level cable on Row 2½, on each cable stitch on Row 4, forming the single flowerettes, and on the top and bottom level cables on the bottom row (Row 5-6) of the 5 step full space wave.

The original design was worked in 2 strands of Marlitt thread No. 1019 (pink) with translucent pink beads by Mill Hill.

This design can be enlarged to a seven row pattern by repeating Rows 3-4 before working the final three rows as Rows 5-7.

The design can be reduced in size by deleting Rows 1 and 5-6.

For a miniature design suitable for dolls, work the design using ½ space pleating threads as full space rows. Use a single bead in the centre of the flowerettes on Row 4 in place of the four beads.

Antique Lace ★★★★
Designer — Sue Batterham

This design looks quite different on a graph compared with the finished product. When the work is completed and blocked out, the design becomes more of an arch shape with a rounded top and points on the lower edge. (See colour plate 2).

It is an ideal choice for garments where less fullness is required, such as a woman's blouse or nightdress, as the surface honeycomb stitch spreads out very well. It is also suitable for smocked collars, bishop style dresses, baby day-gowns and drop waist dresses for both children and adults.

Note: This design uses a combination of surface honeycomb stitch and six cable flowerettes. Note that the four pleats used for the flowerettes are not used in the surface honeycomb stitches but are completely separate. When working the first row (Row 3-5½), it is important to check as you stitch, to make sure you have picked up the correct pleats. Check for 12 free pleats between the lowest points and check your work carefully against the graph before continuing.

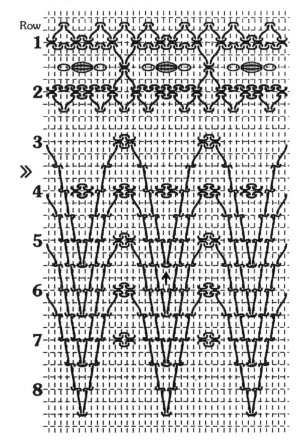

Row ¾	baby wave/3 cable combination over 1/3 of a space
Row 1	11 cable/baby wave combination
Row 2	mirror image of Row 1
Row 2¼	mirror image of Row ¾
≫ Row 3-5½	bottom cable/surface honeycomb/double flowerettes combination with additional double flowerettes on Row 4
Row 4-8½	repeats of bottom cable/surface honeycomb/double flowerettes combination with additional double flowerettes on Row 7
Row 1½	bullion rose buds over 4 pleats with lazy daisy leaves

Centre Row 3-5½; centre stitch — bottom cable Row 5½

Variations:

- The flowerettes on Row 7 could be omitted but may be required to control the fabric where there is a lot of fullness or when a heavy fabric is used.
- As many rows as necessary can be added for a deeper design.
- Flowerettes or lazy daisies may be substituted for rose buds.
- Pearls or beads may be added to flowerettes or to honeycomb stitches.
- Two lengths of very narrow ribbon may be threaded through the top border and tied in a bow (in place of the rose buds).

Colour suggestions:

- This design lends itself to varied shades of one colour, from deepest at the lower edge into paler shades further up. To grade colours more finely you can use one strand of a deeper colour added to one or two strands of a lighter shade etc.
- Soft moss greens or peach in three shades on ivory or white are suggested.
- For a single colour design on adult garments, try silver grey (Marlitt 845) on very pale grey or white fabric or gold (Marlitt 1077) on cream fabric. Tiny matching beads can be added to give some extra interest.

Baby Fiona ★
Designer — Jan Kerton

This design is shown in the colour section on the doll's christening gown and bonnet that was also designed and made by Jan.

A lovely design for baby bishop garments or dolls' clothes. The addition of tiny pearl beads makes this a perfect choice for a christening gown.

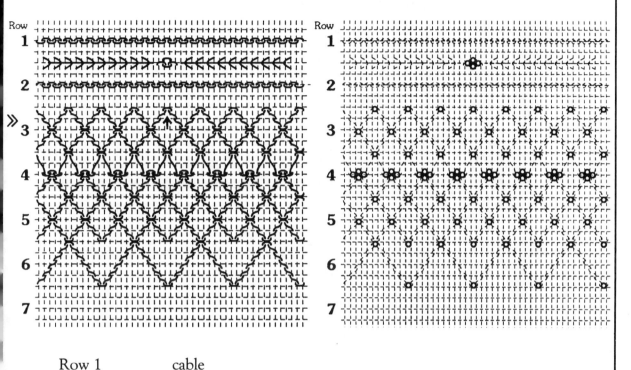

Row 1	cable
Row 2	mirror image of Row 1
Row 1½	raised chain band with central flowerette. Work flowerette first; stitch chain bands towards centre (position as shown on the graph)
≫ Row 2½-3	½ space 2 step wave
Row 3-3½	mirror image of Row 2½-3
Row 3½-4	½ space baby wave/3 cable combination
Row 4-4½	repeat of Row 3-3½
Row 4½-5	repeat of Row 2½-3
Row 5-5½	repeat of Row 3-3½
Row 5½-6½	5 step full space wave. Start in the middle on Row 6½ to ensure centring of the hearts

Centre Row 2½-3; centre stitch — top cable

Refer to graph 2 for bead placement. Where beads are positioned over two adjoining cables, add the beads on the second row.

Original design worked in cream DMC Stranded Cotton; tiny pearl-coloured beads by Mill Hill.

Brittany's Bishop ★★★
Designer — Sue Batterham

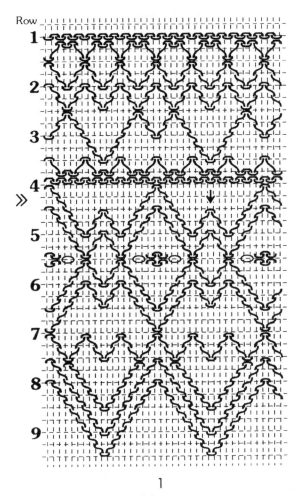

1

Row 1-1½	cable row over ½ space baby wave/3 cable combination
Row 1½-2	2 step ½ space wave
Row 2-2½	repeat Row 1½-2
Row 2½-3½	5 step full space wave/2 step ½ space wave combination
Row 4-3½	mirror image of Row 1-1½
≫ Row 4-5	5 step full space wave/2 step ½ space wave combination
Row 4½-5½	repeat of Row 4-5
Row 5½-6½	mirror image of Row 4½-5½
Row 6½-7½	repeat of Row 5½-6½
Row 7-7½	2 step ½ space wave
Row 7½-8½	5 step wave to form hearts/backsmock across 4 pleats between each repeat
Row 7½-9	8 step 1½ space wave
Row 8-9½	repeat of Row 7½-9
Row 5½	double flowerettes with lazy daisy leaves. Rose buds or bullion roses are other options

Centre Row 4-5; centre stitch — top cable Row 4½

Graph 2 gives a 10 row straight panel version of the design by replacing Rows 7-9½ with a mirror image of Rows 1-4.

Original design worked in DMC Stranded Cotton Nos. 353 (peach), 352 (apricot) and 524 (green).

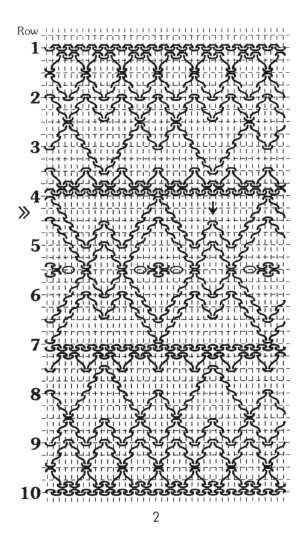

2

Bunnies, Beads and Bows ★★
Designer — Jan Kerton

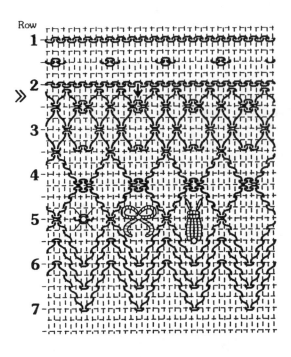

Row 1	cable
Row 2	mirror image of Row 1
≫ Row 2-2½	½ space baby wave/3 cable combination
Row 2½-3	½ space baby wave/3 cable combination
Row 3-3½	mirror image of Row 2½-3
Row 3½-4¼	3 step ¾ space wave/3 cable combination
Row 4¼-5	mirror image of Row 3½-4¼
Row 5-6	4 step full space wave
Row 5½-6½	repeat of Row 5-6
Row 6-7	repeat of Row 5-6
Row 1½	single flowerettes
Row 5	add beaded flowerettes to complete the design; or, for a more advanced design, add the bullion bunnies and/or bows

Centre Row 2-2½; centre stitch — top cable of 3 cable block Row 2½.

Original worked in cream DMC Stranded Cotton.

Beaded flowerettes
Single flowerettes with beads; straight stitches placed on the diagonal with French knot in the centre.

Bunny
Worked on two central pleats in Kanagawa 1000; body middle two bullions — 8 wraps; outer two bullions — 9 wraps; add a wrap stitch at the bottom to pull the bullions together. Head is two bullions of 4 wraps each with lazy daisy ears. Add a white French knot for tail.

Bow
Worked in Silk Stitch; 30 wrap bullions for loops; 25 wrap bullions for tails; French knot for centre.

Carnival ★★★★
Designer — Sue Batterham

An eleven row design with a delightful play of interwoven colours. This design is not difficult to work but care must be taken to complete the first stage accurately before starting the second stage.

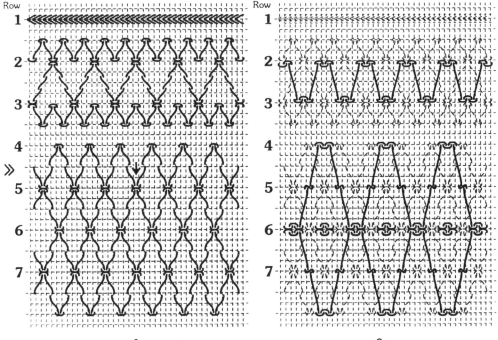

1   2

Stage 1 — Graph 1

Row 1	stem/outline stitch
Row 1½-2	baby wave; centre bottom cable to line up with centre bottom cable of Row 4-5
Row 2-3	3 step full space wave
Row 3-3½	mirror image of Row 1½-2
≫ Row 4-5	2 step full space wave (note that top level cables Row 4 do *not* line up with bottom level cables of Row 3½)
Row 5-6	mirror image of Row 4-5
Rows 6-11	mirror image of Rows 1-6

Centre Row 4-5; centre stitch — bottom cable Row 5

Stage 2 — Graph 2

Row 2-3	full space chevron with 3 cables top & bottom
Row 4-6	2 space 2 step chevron with cable at step on Row 5 and 3 cables top & bottom
Rows 6-10	mirror image of Rows 2-6
Row 6	double flowerettes

Variations:

Fifteen row design can be created by repeating Rows 4-8 to double the centre panel. Bottom border will start at Row 12½.

To create a bishop design, delete Rows 7-11 from stage 1 and delete Row 9-10 from stage 2.

This design is ideal for a plain insert in a tartan or floral fabric and lends itself to strong bright colours, making it suitable for boys garments.

Original design worked in DMC Stranded Cotton Nos. 597 (aqua), 961 (hot pink) and 744 (yellow).

Other suggested colour combinations:

- red, white and green on black fabric
- red, yellow and white on navy fabric
- black, white and deep pink on hot pink fabric

Hearts and Flowers ★★★
Designer — Jan Kerton

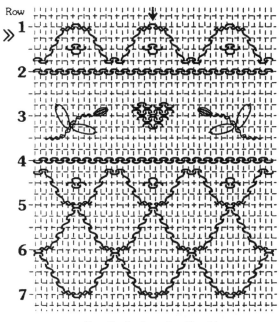

Row 3 - backsmock with cable

1

Graph 1 — Bishop Design

≫ Row 1-1¾	3 cables/3 step wave scallop-up combination
Row 2	cable
Row 3	backsmock with cable
Row 4	mirror image of Row 2
Row 4¼-5	mirror image of Row 1-1¾
Row 5-6	full space 4 step wave scallop-down
Row 6-7	full space 4 step wave scallop-down
Row 3	add rose buds and hearts
Rows 1½ & 4½	work single flowerettes

Centre Row 1-1¾; centre stitch — top cable Row 1

Details of flower design follow at the end of Straight Yoke Design.

Original design worked in DMC Stranded Cotton Nos. 224 (pink), 504 (green), 677 (gold), 932 (blue) and 3042 (mauve).

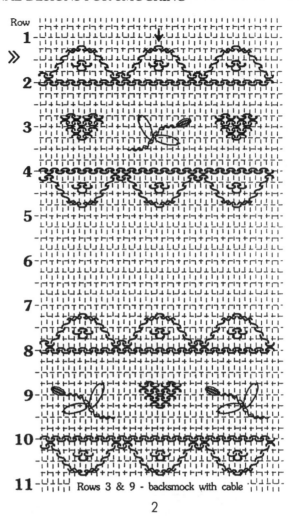

2

Graph 2 — Straight Yoke Design

≫ Row 1¼-2	3 cables/3 step wave scallop-up combination
Row 2	cable
Row 3	backsmock with cable
Row 4	mirror image of Row 2
Row 4-4¾	mirror image of Row 1¼-2
Rows 7¼-10¾	repeat Rows 1¼-4¾
Rows 3 & 9	embroider hearts and flowers

Centre Row 1¼-2; centre stitch — top cable Row 1¼

Add single flowerettes in all scallops.

Note that the fabric will puff between Rows 5 & 7 when the pleating threads are removed.

Original design worked in DMC Stranded Cotton Nos. 335 (dark pink), 368 (green), 776 (pale pink) and 3752 (blue).

Flower details

For the flowers pointing up and to the right, work in stem stitch; three on the line, three up ½ space, then three on the line. For the flowers pointing up and to the left, work in outline stitch; three on the line, three down ½ space, then three on the line. Complete with bullion rose buds over 3 pleats and lazy daisy leaves.

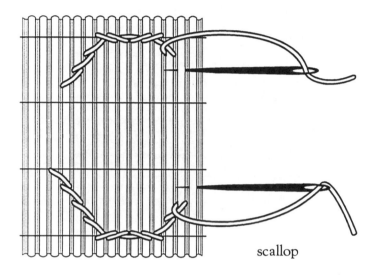

scallop

Kaleidoscope ★★★
Designer — Jan Kerton

This design is shown in the colour section on the floral dress that was also designed and made by Jan.

This dense design is full of colour and suitable for overall prints, such as Liberty, but would be equally effective in bright colours on a plain background for boys' garments.

The original design was worked in DMC Stranded Cotton, but if you want even greater contrast on overall prints, try working with a high gloss thread such as Marlitt.

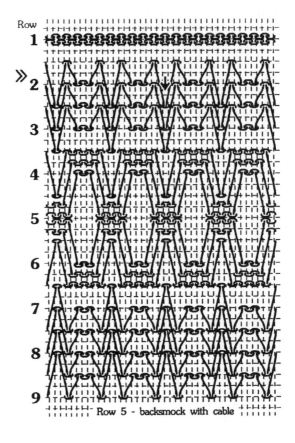

Row 5 - backsmock with cable

Row 1	2 rows of cable (stacked)
≫ Row 1½-2½	3 cable/½ space chevron/full space chevron combination
Row 2-3	repeat Row 1½-2½
Row 2½-3½	repeat Row 1½-2½
Row 3½-4½	7 cable/full space chevron combination
Row 3¾-4¾	5 cable/full space chevron with 3 cable combination
Row 4-5	3 cable/full space chevron with 5 cable combination
Row 5	backsmock with cable
Rows 5-8½	mirror image of Rows 1½-5
Row 8-9	repeat of Row 7½-8½

Centre Row 1½-2½; centre stitch — bottom level stitch Row 2½

Original design worked in DMC Stranded Cotton Nos. 726 (yellow), 3687 (pink), 792 (blue) and 991 (green).

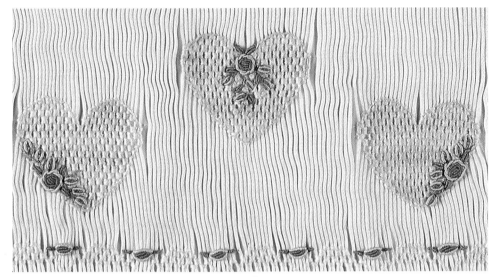

WITH LOVE

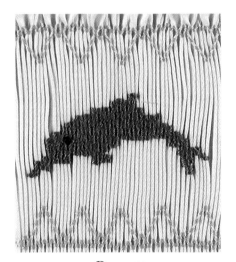

DOLPHIN

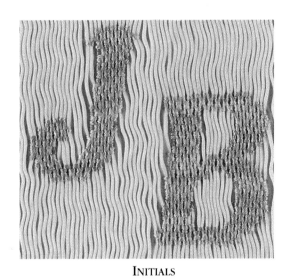

INITIALS

BUTTERFLIES

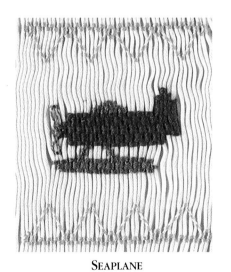

SEAPLANE

PLATE 5 — STACKING DESIGNS

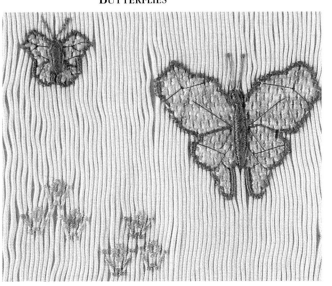

SUN DRESS, FEATURING BUTTERFLIES DESIGN, AND
PEASANT DRESS, FEATURING KAREN DESIGN

TARTAN DRESS, FEATURING PRACTICAL PLAIDS SMOCKING DESIGN

DOLL'S DRESS AND BONNET, FEATURING BABY FIONA, AND
MATCHING PILLOW, FEATURING LAURA

FLORAL DRESS, FEATURING KALEIDOSCOPE SMOCKING DESIGN

DRESS, FEATURING DECORATIVE BACK SMOCKING, AND BLOUSE AND
MATCHING COATHANGER, FEATURING COUNTERCHANGE SMOCKING

SMOCKED DRESS YOKE AND CREAM BLOUSE YOKE

Karen ★★
Designer — Jenny Bradford

Pictured on the peasant style dress made by Jenny.

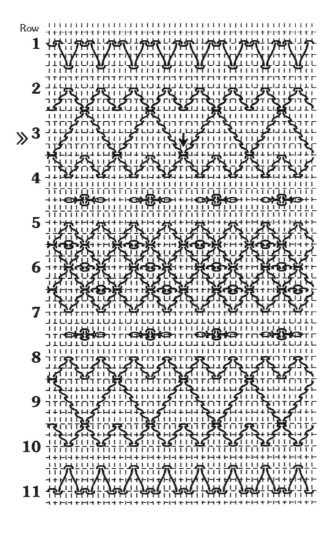

Row 1-1½	3 cables/½ space chevron combination
Row 2-2½	2 step ½ space wave
≫ Row 2½-3½	5 step full space wave
Row 3½-4	mirror image of Row 2-2½
Row 4½	double flowerettes with lazy daisy leaves
Row 5-5½	repeat of Row 2-2½
Row 5½-6	mirror image of Row 5-5½
Row 6-6½	repeat of Row 5-5½
Row 6½-7	repeat of Row 5½-6

Row 7½	repeat of Row 4½
Row 8-8½	repeat of Row 2-2½
Row 8½-9½	mirror image of Row 2½-3½
Row 9½-10	repeat of Row 3½-4
Row 10½-11	mirror image of Row 1-1½

Centre Row 2½-3½; centre stitch — bottom cable Row 3½

Ribbon can be threaded through Row 1-1½ and Row 10½-11.
Single flowerettes are worked in diagonal rows across the diamond pattern. The pattern can be varied by altering the placement of these flowerettes.

This design can be enlarged by repeating the bands of design as shown on the peasant style dress pictured in the colour section.
The diamond band between Rows 5 & 7 can also be extended by an even number of rows, e.g. by 2 rows over one full space or 4 rows over 2 full spaces.
The original design is worked in cream, apricot and pale green Au Ver à Soie stranded silk.

Laura ★★★★
Designer — Jan Kerton

This is a lovely design featuring ribbon threading, beading and silk ribbon embroidery. A great choice for a special occasion dress, or a keepsake ring pillow for a bride.
Bullion rose embroidery can be substituted for the ribbon embroidery or replace the embroidery with tiny lace motifs of butterflies, birds, bows or hearts etc. (available from embroidery or bridal shops). The tiny stacked butterfly pictured on colour plate 5 could also be used.

Row 1	cable
Row 1½-2	½ space chevron for ribbon threading
≫ Row 2½-3½	3 step wave/stem stitch combination with a bead threaded on each stitch. (If beads are not used, replace stem stitch with outline stitch, following each upper wave as shown in the graph)
Row 4-4½	½ space chevron
Row 4½-5	mirror image of Row 4-4½

Row 5-5½ &	(worked as one row; pass needle behind work from Row 5 to
Row 3½-4	Row 4 as indicated by the dotted line on the graph) ½ space chevron to form diamonds
Row 5½-6	½ space chevron to complete top half of pattern as shown on the graph
Row 6	backsmock with cable
Rows 6-11	mirror image of Rows 1-6

Centre Row 2½-3½; centre stitch — top level stitch Row 2½

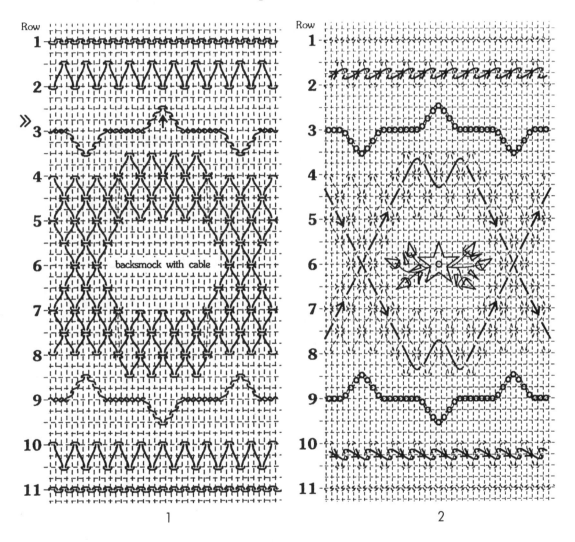

Refer to graph 2 for details of ribbon threading and embroidery design.

The silk ribbon embroidery for the buds and the daisy shown is worked in bullion lazy daisy stitch with stranded silk bullion lazy daisy leaves. Further information on silk ribbon embroidery can be found in my books *Silk Ribbon Embroidery for Gifts and Garments* and *Original Designs for Silk Ribbon Embroidery*.

Original design worked in DMC Stranded Cotton Nos. 747 (blue), 963 (pink) and 745 (yellow). Beads are Mill Hill No. 2001 (yellow).

Lisa ★★
Designer — Jenny Bradford

This is a simple design that can be enlarged by alternating the bands as desired. Substitute double flowerettes for the rose buds if you find bullion rose buds difficult.

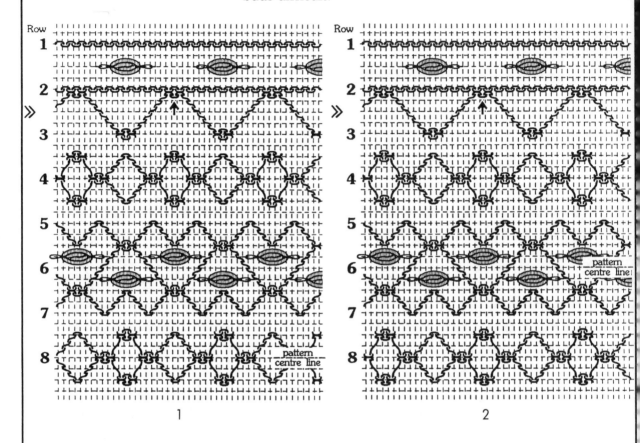

Graph 1: 15 row version as illustrated in colour

Row 1	cable
Row 2	mirror image of Row 1
≫ Row 2-3	6 step full space wave with double flowerettes at Row 3 and 3 cable at Row 2 to form double flowerettes
Row 3½-4	½ space chevron/double flowerettes/3 cable/3 step ½ space wave combination
Row 4-4½	mirror image of Row 3½-4
Row 5-5½	3 step ½ space wave/3 cable combination
Row 5½-6½	6 step full space wave/3 cable combination

Row 6½-7	3 step ½ space wave/3 cable combination
Row 7½-8	½ space chevron/double flowerettes/3 cable/3 step ½ space wave combination
Row 8-8½	mirror image of Row 7½-8
Rows 9-15	mirror image of Rows 1-7

Centre Row 2-3; centre line — bottom cable Row 2

Add rose buds or double flowerettes as shown.

Graph 2: 11 row version

Rows 1-7	as for 15 row version
Rows 7½-11	mirror image of Rows 1-4½

Original design worked in Marlitt No. 1019 (pink). Rose buds worked in Silk Stitch Nos. 140 (pink) and 190 (dark pink).

Margaret ★★★

Designer — Jenny Bradford

This type of design works most effectively when the grid of diamonds is worked in a colour closely matched to the background fabric.

The centre panel of the design can be adjusted to fill any depth. (See centre panel of Karen for a small version based on the same idea.)

The combinations of bullion stitches and flowerettes is unlimited, making it a simple exercise to work your own adaptation of the idea. Satin stitches can be substituted for the bullion stitches or flowerettes if preferred.

An easy way to design your own adaptation is to work the foundation grid, take a photocopy and then experiment with coloured pencils on tracing paper over the grid to position the bullions, flowerettes or satin stitches.

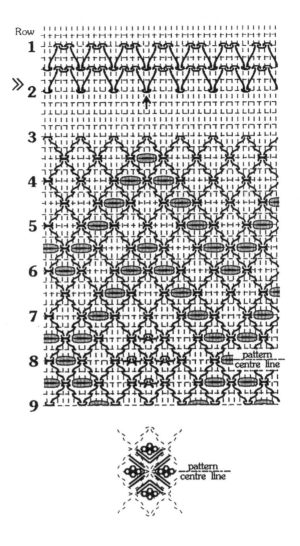

≫ Row 1-1½   3 cable/½ space chevron combination
  Row 1½-2   repeat Row 1-1½
  Row 3-3½   ½ space 2 step wave
  Row 3½-4   mirror image of Row 3-3½ to form diamonds
  Rows 4-13   repeat Rows 3-4 nine times
  Rows 14-15   mirror image of Rows 1-2

Centre Row 1-1½; centre stitch — bottom level stitch Row 1½

Using a single strand of Marlitt thread or Silk Stitch, work the bullion stitch pattern to form the design.

   Add flowerettes. In each of the 4 centre diamonds add beads to each stitch of the flowerettes and place 4 bullions in a V pointing to the centre of the design (as shown in the detail drawing).

   Original design is worked in Marlitt Nos. 1042 (peach), 1052 (aqua) and 1013 (gold).

Pattie ★★
Designer — Jenny Bradford

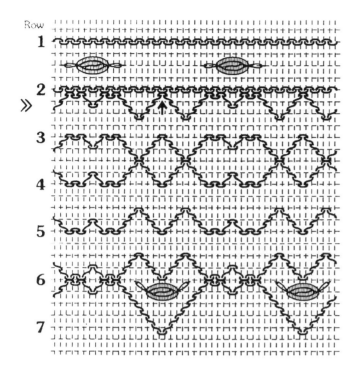

Row 1	cable
Row 2	mirror image of Row 1
≫ Row 2-2½	3 step wave/3 cable/¼ space chevron combination
Row 3-3½	repeat of Row 2-2½
Rows 3½-5	mirror image of Rows 2-3½
Row 5½-6	repeat of Row 4½-5
Row 6-7	7 step full space wave (to form hearts)/3 cable/¼ space chevron combination

Centre Row 2-2½; centre stitch — middle top level stitch Row 2 of three step wave

Work rose buds or double flowerettes as desired.
   Original design worked in Marlitt No. 1052 (aqua). Rose buds worked in Silk Stitch Nos. 140 (pale pink) and 190 (deep pink).

Baby Pattie ★★

A tiny version of Pattie suitable for working on half space pleating for tiny doll garments

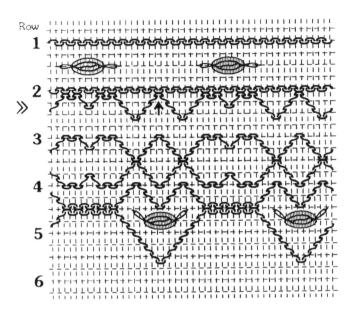

Rows 1-4	same as Rows 1-4 of Pattie
Row 4-4½	9 cable/3 step ½ space wave combination
Row 4½-5	9 cable/7 step full space wave to form hearts

Work rose buds or double flowerettes as preferred.

Pauline ★★★

Designer — Jenny Bradford

This design has a pretty effect, as it dips lower in the front of a bishop style garment, showing the maximum amount of smocking where it will have the maximum effect.

It is ideally suited to a woman's bishop style nightgown. However it can be reduced in depth by working fewer rows of two step wave at the row 2½ to 4 level. It is also possible to work on half space pleating for a doll design.

The finish at the top neck edge is designed to work without a neck binding. The ribbon is adjusted to hold the neck gathers in place on a garment with a lower neck edge that does not require an opening.

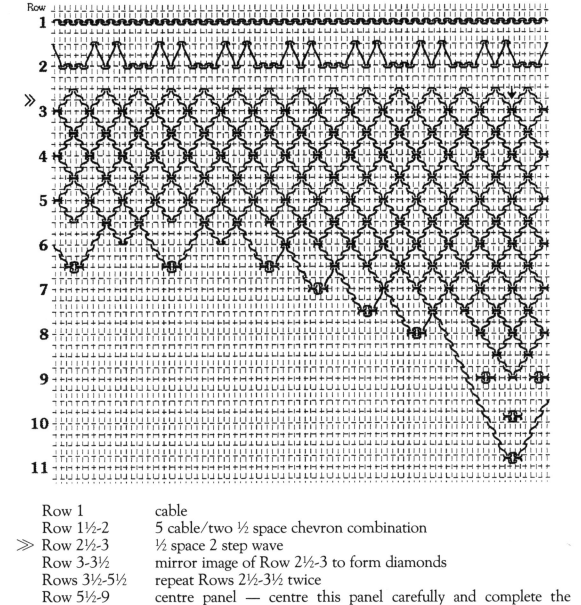

Row 1	cable
Row 1½-2	5 cable/two ½ space chevron combination
≫ Row 2½-3	½ space 2 step wave
Row 3-3½	mirror image of Row 2½-3 to form diamonds
Rows 3½-5½	repeat Rows 2½-3½ twice
Row 5½-9	centre panel — centre this panel carefully and complete the diamond design, working backward and forward across this centre panel until the single wave is completed on Row 8½-9
Row 5½-11	commence at the centre of the front panel, following the graph carefully to work the uneven steps, starting with a 13 step 3¼ space wave. Half space 2 step wave & 5 step full space wave, forming alternate diamonds and hearts, complete Row 5½-6½

Centre Row 2½-3; centre stitch — lower level stitch Row 3.

The double flowerettes worked in the centre front space may be replaced by bullion roses or silk ribbon embroidery.

Original design worked in white DMC Stranded Cotton.

Tudor Rose ★★★
Designer — Sue Batterham

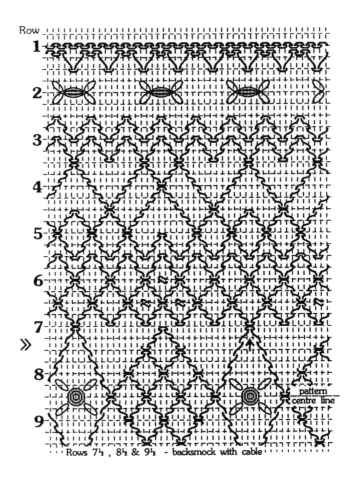

Rows 7½, 8½ & 9½ - backsmock with cable

Row 1	cable
Row 1-1½	cable (form double flowerettes)/ ½ space chevron combination
Row 2½-3	2 step ½ space wave
Row 3-3½	repeat Row 2½-3
Row 3½-4½	5 step full space wave/2 step ½ space wave combination
Row 4-5	2 step ½ space wave/5 step full space wave combination
Row 5-5½	½ space 2 step wave
Row 5½-6	repeat of Row 5-5½
Row 6-6½	mirror image of Row 5½-6
Row 6½-7	repeat of Row 5½-6
≫ Row 7-8½	5 step full space wave/2 step ½ space wave combination

Row 7-8	2 step ½ space wave to complete diamond shapes
Row 7½ & 8½	backsmock with cable
Rows 8½-16	mirror image of Rows 1-8½

Complete design with:

Row 2 & 15	bullion rose buds over 4 pleats with lazy daisy leaves
Row 6, 6½, 10½ & 11	2 satin stitches over centre pleats in diamonds as marked on the graph
Row 8-9	bullion roses with lazy daisy leaves

Centre Row 7-8½; centre stitch — top level stitch Row 7

Variations:

For a deeper pattern, add extra rows of two step wave between Rows 6 & 7 and between Rows 10 & 11. Double flowerettes can be substituted for rose buds or bullion roses. Three rose buds can be substituted for the large bullion roses.

Original design worked in DMC Stranded Cotton Nos. 316 (rose), 3042 (lavender) and 778 (pink) with satin stitches in 316, rose buds in 316, 778 and 522 (green) and bullion roses in 316, 778, 522 and Semco 859 (dark rose).

SMOCKING PLAIDS

Sue Batterham has evolved this easy way of simulating plaids in smocking. Unlike some methods of representing plaid designs, there is no double pick-up of pleats, as the colours cross over, making this method simple and easy to work.

Tartan designs are wonderful for smocking plain fabric as the choices and combinations of colours are endless. Your garment could also be trimmed with tartan fabric, from which you can choose the colours for smocking (see colour plate). Touches of an additional colour can easily be added by working flowerettes, satin stitches or bullion stitches in the unsmocked diamond areas and in a wider border design.

Suggested uses for Smocking Plaids:
- boys' garments
- child's pinafore teamed with a tartan blouse
- girl's or woman's drop waist dress
- insert in coat, jacket or wind-cheater
- insert in the shoulder line of a blouse
- yoke dress
- decorative bands, cuffs and pockets
- cushions and bags

WORKING YOUR OWN DESIGN

The number of pleated rows used can be varied from about seven up to as many as you wish.

The pattern is worked diagonally across the fabric in groups of 3, 5 or 7 rows.

A three row grouping will result in a small pattern suitable for smaller garments, whilst a seven row grouping should only be used on deep panels, as the pattern is correspondingly larger.

The sample design, Practical Plaids, illustrates a five row grouping using three colours in the sequence of blue, red, yellow, red, blue.

Use a separate needle for each colour to avoid constant re-threading as each colour is needed.

Stage 1

With the thread *below* the needle, start from the lower left with a bottom level stitch, then, keeping the thread below the needle, move up a ½ space and work another bottom level stitch over the next two pleats to the right (see Stitch Glossary — Half Space Chevron Diagonal). Repeat at each ½ space to the top of the plaid.

Each row in the 3, 5 or 7 row group is started three pleats to the right of the preceding row, i.e. leave two unsmocked pleats between each row.

Leave six unsmocked pleats between each group of 3, 5 or 7 rows (see graph 1 of Practical Plaids).

Continue across the fabric.

To fill in the top left hand corner, keep the same colour sequence and start each row of the group one full space up on the left hand edge.

Leave a gap equal to two pleating thread spaces between each group of rows (to give six unsmocked pleats between the groups — see graph 1 of Practical Plaids.)

Stage 2

With the thread *above* the needle and starting from the top, at each half space mark, work top level stitches, in a downward diagonal direction across the stage 1 stitching. Begin the pattern with the first colour by picking up the two pleats immediately to the left of the first colour of the first group in stage 1. Each subsequent row of the group will commence by taking up the two free pleats left between rows in stage 1. The six unsmocked pleats left between the groups in stage 1 will be reduced to four by completion of stage 2.

Fill in the lower left hand corner in the same way as described in stage 1, working down the left hand edge instead of up.

Practical Plaids ★★★
Designer — Sue Batterham

Pictured in the colour section on a dress designed and made by Sue.

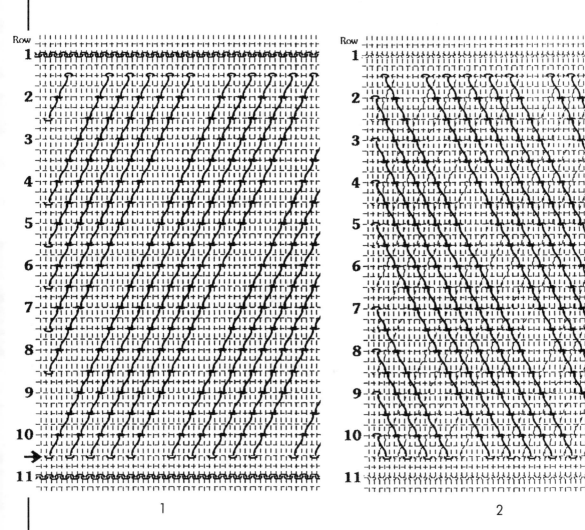

1

2

Stage 1 — Graph 1
Row 1   cable
Rows 1½-10½   diagonal ½ space baby wave,
                   working from bottom to top
Row 11   cable

Stage 2 — Graph 2
Repeat of Stage 1 Rows 1½-10½, but working from top to bottom.
    Original worked in DMC Stranded Cotton in red, blue and yellow.

STACKING DESIGNS FOR PICTURE SMOCKING

Designer — Jenny Bradford

This is a method of creating pictorial designs by working from a chart and 'stacking' cable stitches in such a way that they cover the fabric to create the desired shape.

Stacking refers to the way in which the stitches are worked in order to cover the background fabric. Cable stitches are worked close together, with the top level stitches of the row being directly under the bottom level stitches of the row above.

It is important to achieve the right proportion with the stitches, otherwise the picture may look distorted. Easy designs for the beginner are such items as balloons, as any slight variation in the height and width will not adversely affect the finished design. Small animals and figures will require greater accuracy to achieve perfect results.

The weight of the fabric chosen is important as it will affect the horizontal size of the design. I think stacking designs work the best on an average weight cotton fabric that has sufficient body to support the weight of the stitching. A voile or batiste fabric will pleat more closely and therefore reduce the width of the design. In this case, the vertical size of a design must also be adjusted by using fewer strands of thread for stitching. The overall effect of this will be to decrease the size of the pictures worked in the design.

On an average weight fabric three or four strands of stranded cotton or silk will give the best results. The finished results of the stitching will depend on successful handling of the thread and good tension of the stitching.

Backsmocking is an integral part of picture work and I find it quicker, easier and safer to backsmock the complete panel before starting the picture work. This method ensures that no unsightly gaps occur between the backsmocking and picture work due to missed pleats. It also means that the pleating threads can be relaxed slightly after the backsmocking is completed, ensuring that the stacking will not be worked too tightly.

Match the thread to the background fabric and work with two strands of stranded cotton or Perlé No. 8. Take care not to stitch too deeply when backsmocking to avoid unsightly stitches showing on the surface or interfering with the stacking to be worked later. Backsmocking should create a shadow on the surface but the stitching should not show in any way. For stacking designs, cable, wave or diamond designs can be used to create attractive shadow patterns on which to base the picture design.

The following points will help you to master the technique of picture smocking, which is not unduly difficult but does require care and attention to detail.

- Allow sufficient fabric; picture work does not stretch as much as regular smocking.

- Backsmock first then slacken the pleating threads a little and block, so that the stacking can be worked without requiring further stretching on completion.

- Work a small sample to establish the required number of threads to give the correct number of rows depicted on the pattern (usually about 4 or 5 rows to one pleating thread space). When working the cables it is important to allow sufficient space between each row to permit the threads to lay smoothly and not overlap each other or leave a gap to show base fabric through the design. Overlapping threads will have a lumpy appearance and detract from the overall finish. Be sure to strip the thread before threading the needle and take care to lay each stitch carefully to avoid the threads crossing over each other as each stitch is formed. Watch the tension carefully and do not pull the stitches too tightly. The finish should look like little satin stitched bricks in a wall.

- To ensure the design is worked straight, where possible always start with one of the longest rows centred over a pleating thread.

- To make the design easier to follow, you can take a photocopy and colour in the first and every alternate row with a highlight pen (or colour in the original charts if you wish). These rows will be worked with the work and the chart the right way up; the remaining rows will be worked with the work and the chart turned upside down. Mark off each row as it is completed and you will always know exactly where you are up to. (It is all too easy to lose the place and miscount the stitches.)

- Half stitches are often used to fill in gaps at the end of the rows. These are satin stitches worked over one pleat to keep the edge of the design smooth.

- The outline of the shape can be further accentuated by working a row of outline or stem stitch and satin stitch using two or three strands of thread around the outer edge of the shape. Where this method is used, it is not necessary to fill in all the half stitches at the start and finish of the rows; the outline stitches can be used to fill the gaps (as in the butterfly and heart designs).

The stacking designs detailed here are intended to be used in a variety of ways. They can be worked in a regular pattern as shown in the heart design. The large butterflies, dolphins or seaplanes could all be used in this way.

A more individual interpretation of the motifs is shown in the butterfly pattern where large and small butterflies have been mixed in the design. Initials together with some tiny butterflies would make an interesting pocket design. Dolphins could be worked as if swimming in a group rather than following each other single file across a panel.

Note: In all the diagrams the horizontal lines represent pleating threads and the vertical lines are drawn at ten pleats spacing.

Alphabet ★★

The letters are intended to be used as initials, or a full name across a panel, which could be used on dungarees, sweat shirts, cushion and bag panels or pockets. When working a name across a panel be careful to ensure that all the letters are on the right level.

The letters could be embellished with embroidery using bullion stitch or silk ribbon flowers.

The original initials are worked in variegated threads but the possibilities are endless to suit the application of the design.

If outline stitching is not used, it will be necessary to add half stitches to fill in gaps at the end of rows.

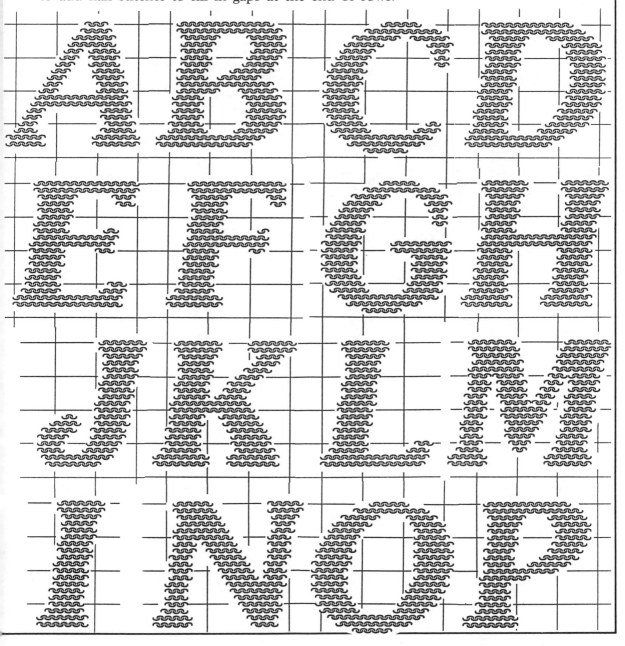

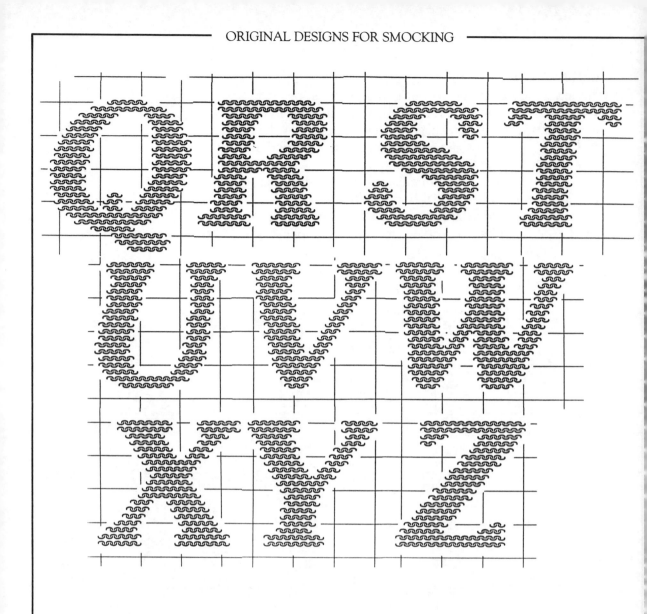

Butterfly — large ★★★

This design is shown in the colour section on a child's sun dress made by Jenny.

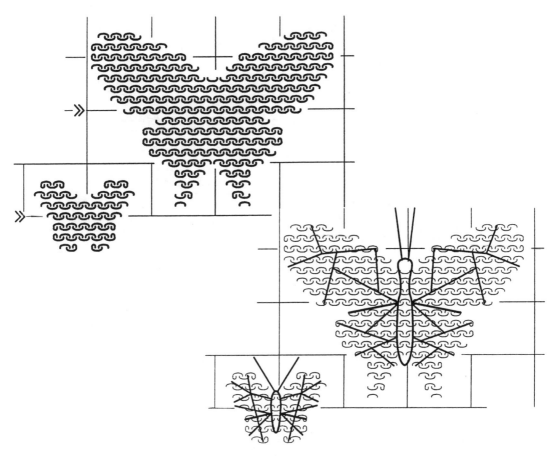

Worked across 39 pleats by 3½ spaces deep.

- Start with the row indicated, with 27 cable stitches. Build up the design above and below this base line as described previously and following the chart carefully.

- Using a single strand of brown thread, couch an outline for the body as shown on chart 2. Using 2 strands, fill in this shape with long vertical stitches for padding before working satin stitch across the outlined area to complete the body shape. Couch the outline again to smooth the shape.

- The fine vein lines shown on the second chart are worked in straight stitch in a fine metallic thread, a single strand of embroidery thread or machine embroidery thread.

- Feelers are a single straight stitch with a colonial knot on the end.

Butterfly — small ★★★

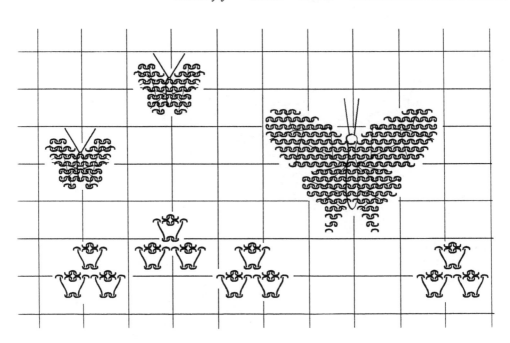

Worked across 17 pleats by 1½ spaces deep.

This butterfly is worked in exactly the same way as the large butterfly, commencing with 11 cables on the starting row. Variegated threads are an excellent choice for the butterflies.

Dolphin ★★

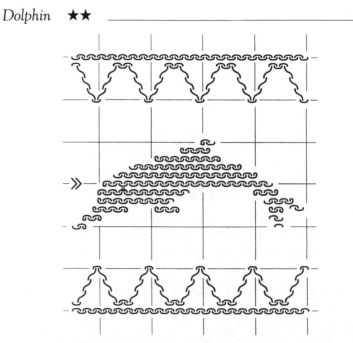

Worked across 45 pleats by 2 spaces deep.

Commence with ½ cable, 32 cable, ½ cable across the starting row. Follow the graph carefully. Use a colonial knot or tiny black bead for the eye.

Original design worked in DMC Stranded Cotton No. 414 (grey).

Hearts 'My Love' ★★

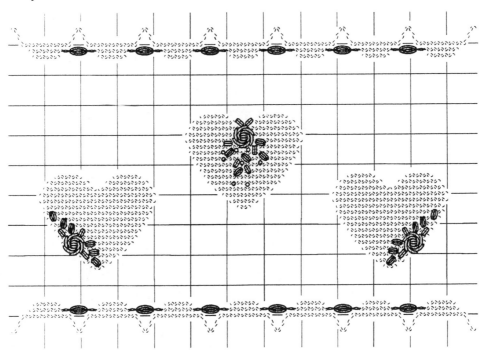

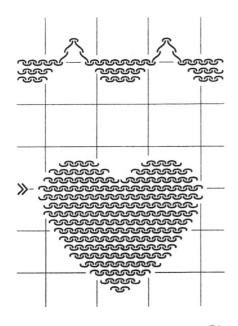

Worked across 32 pleats by 3 spaces deep.

This design makes an excellent beginner's project, the border design providing good practice in stacking for the inexperienced.

The hearts are decorated with tiny bullion roses and rose buds. A single heart could be used as a pocket motif or the hearts could be scattered at random over the bodice of a dress on a larger panel.

Commence each heart with 31 cables across the starting row as indicated and follow the graph row by row.

The edge of each heart is worked with outline and stem stitch; work the stitches to fit snugly around the edge, filling in the spaces at the start and finish of each row.

Work the embroidery as shown on the graph or to your own design. The original embroidery is worked in Silk Stitch as it is an easier thread to use for bullion embroidery than stranded cotton.

Original design worked in variegated stranded cotton in pale pink and pale blue; embroidery in Silk Stitch Nos. 140 (pale pink), 170 (dusty pink) and 113 (green).

The Border

Row 1	2 step ½ space wave/13 cable combination
Row 2	9 cable stacked across centre of 13 cable group. Backsmock across the gap between each group
Row 3	7 cable stacked under the 9 cable block. Backsmock across the gap as before

Work bullion rose buds across six pleats between each scallop.

Sea Plane ★★ _____

This simple little design works well on a little boy's shirt or a small pocket. It can also be worked into a larger panel design by positioning several planes each in a different colour across the panel.

Commencing with 27½ cable stitches across the row indicated, complete the 4 rows for the body and the tail of the aircraft in one colour. Work the cockpit, struts and floats in grey. Work the propeller with two strands of grey thread as follows:

- Bring the needle up at A and down at B.
- Come back up at C and take a backstitch from B to C.
- Take the needle across from C to D, go down at D and come back up at A.
- Backstitch D to A.

Repeat for the other half of the propeller.

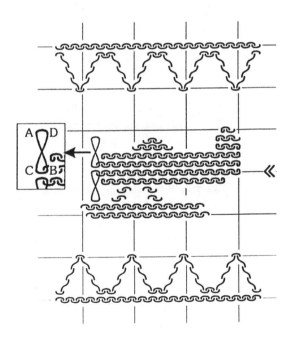

CHAPTER FOUR

STITCH GLOSSARY

The small diagrams accompanying the stitch diagrams in this section depict the same stitches in the way they are shown in the design plate diagrams.

CABLE STITCH

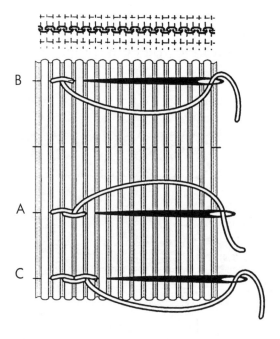

A straight line stitch.

A top level cable is formed by keeping the thread *above* the needle when you are picking up the pleat (diagram A).

A bottom level cable is formed by keeping the thread *below* the needle when you are picking up the pleat (diagram B).

A row of cables is made up of alternate top and bottom level stitches (diagram C).

CHEVRON

HALF SPACE CHEVRON OR BABY WAVE

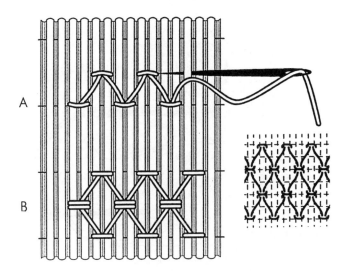

Work a bottom level cable, move up ½ space and pick up the next pleat (diagram A) and work a top level cable.

Working a mirror image of the first row will create chevron diamonds (diagram B).

Note: To keep diamonds even, allow for the space taken up by the thread when judging spacing and needle position. On diagram B a ½ space pleating thread would pass between the cables where they meet in the centre of the row. The top and bottom cables just touch the full space threads but do not encroach on the next spaces.

FULL SPACE CHEVRON

This is worked in exactly the same way, picking up on the full space instead of the ½ space mark.

DOUBLE SPACE TWO STEP CHEVRON

Extra cables can be worked at the top and/or bottom level to form a variety of combination stitches.

HALF SPACE CHEVRON DIAGONAL

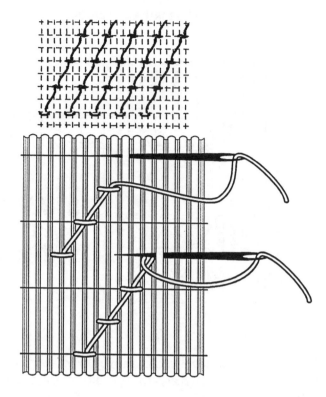

Work in half space steps, keeping the thread *below* the needle as you travel up the work and *above* the needle as you travel down the work.

OUTLINE AND STEM STITCH

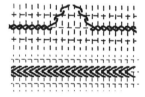

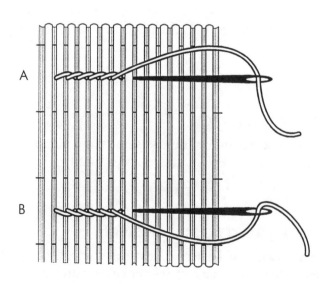

A

B

Outline is worked across the pleats, keeping the thread *above* the needle on every stitch (diagram A).

Stem stitch is the same as outline stitch but worked with the thread *below* the needle on every stitch (diagram B).

RAISED CHAIN STITCH

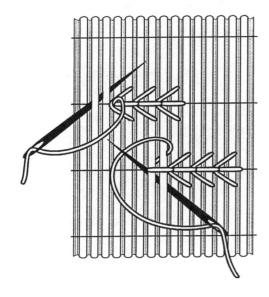

Work from *right* to *left* or turn the work so that the pleats are horizontal, and work from top to bottom.

SURFACE HONEYCOMB

This is one of the few smocking stitches where the same pleat is picked up twice in the stitching process.

After working the first level cable, pick up the second pleat used in that cable the required ½ or full space distance away and work the next cable.

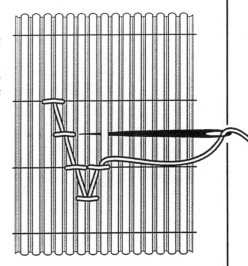

TRELLIS OR WAVE STITCH

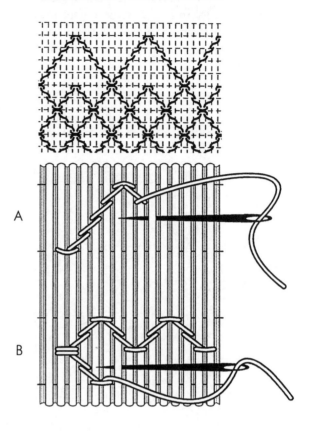

A

B

This stitch is one of the most common used in smocking and may be referred to by either name. The basic rule for working these and all other zigzag stitches is that the thread is held *below* the needle for the bottom level stitch and when working in an upward direction and *above* the needle for the top level stitch and when working in a downward direction.

Waves can be worked over any distance from ¼ space to any number of spaces. The number of steps detailed in the pattern dictates the spacing required to cover that distance. Diagram A shows a four step full space wave. Diagram B shows two rows of two step ½ space waves to form diamonds. The second row is often detailed in instructions as a *mirror image* of the first row.

Extra cables can be worked at the top and bottom level, which, when matched up with other rows, may form single or double flowerettes.

VAN DYKE STITCH

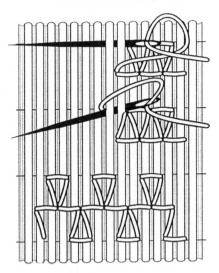

Worked from *right* to *left*.

Each pleat is picked up twice and the top and bottom level stitches are created by backstitching two pleats together. It can be worked in a straight line, waves or on the diagonal, as shown in the diagram.

THREE PLEAT VAN DYKE STITCH

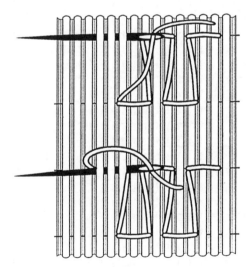

This stitch creates an interesting texture on the surface of the fabric when worked as backsmocking. No stitching will show on the surface, which can be further embellished with beads or embroidery.

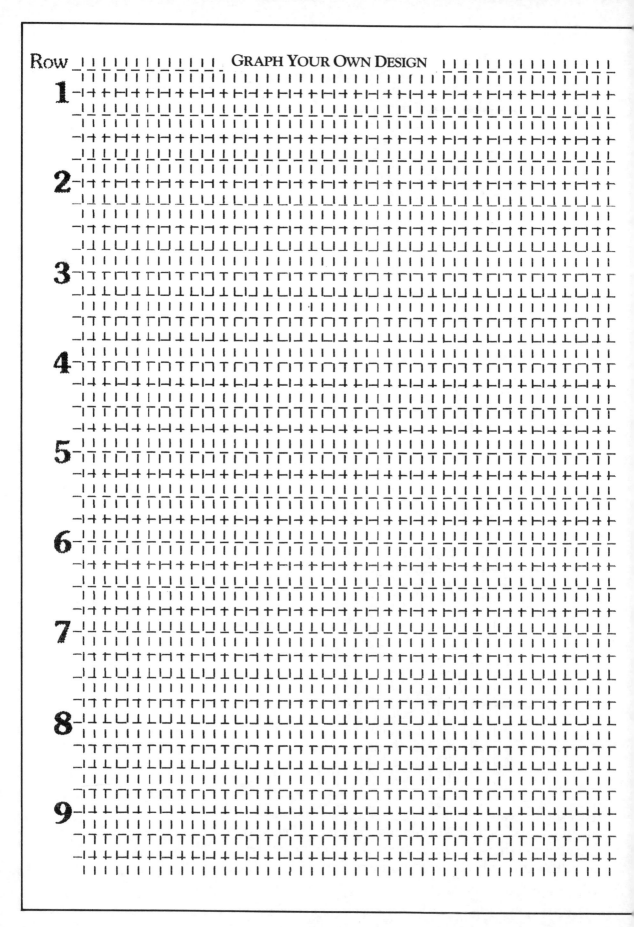

Row GRAPH YOUR OWN DESIGN

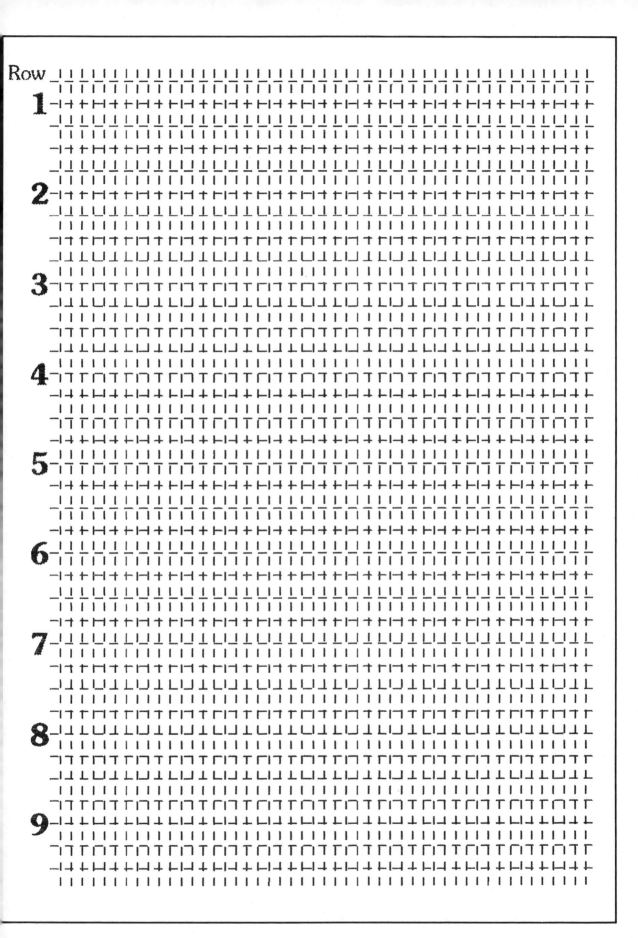

Row
1
2
3
4
5
6
7
8
9